The Dust Catcher

The Dust Catcher 

and other poems

Marjorie Sparkman Jackson

2010 · FITHIAN PRESS
McKINLEYVILLE, CALIFORNIA

"City Park" was previously published in *The Archer*.
Cover photo: "Moon Goddess Looks Down," by Dennis Roth
   www.oozingthemoon.com

Published by Fithian Press
A division of Daniel and Daniel, Publishers, Inc.
Post Office Box 2790
McKinleyville, CA 95519
www.danielpublishing.com

Distributed by SCB Distributors (800) 729-6423

LIBRARY OF CONGRESS CATALOGING-IN-PUBLICATION DATA
Jackson, Marjorie Sparkman, (date)
 The dust catcher, and other poems / by Marjorie Sparkman Jackson.
    p. cm.
 ISBN 978-1-56474-501-9 (pbk. : alk. paper)
 1. Supernatural—-Poetry. I. Title.
 PS3610.A3543D87 2010
 811'.6--dc22
        2010015667

*By heaven, I do love: and it hath taught me
to rhyme, and to be melancholy.*

(Shakespeare, *Love's Labour's Lost)*

To Foster David Sparkman

Contents

— *Part One* —

Thereby hangs a tale.

(Shakespeare, *As You Like It*)

In Salem Village

On Gallows Hill in sixteen ninety-two,
the innocents were hanged before their God
to prove the circumspection of their peers.

They did not sleep beneath the unblessed sod,
unhallowed ground gives up its angry bones
and spills out here a hand, out there a chin.

True witches they were not, yet still they moan
on moonlit nights when clouds are low and thin
and restless dogs are whimpering in fear.

The Old Well

The old well out in the south pasture
was on the same path going to the woods.
It's long since been abandoned
since we got city water from the town.
But I think of it from time to time,
how good it used to taste, fresh and cold.

The well's been covered since sixty-two
and no one remembers why, except me.

Twenty years ago a little girl got lost,
and the whole countryside was looking
through the hills, the woods, the fields,
but to no good. Finally, after a while,
they told her little brother she'd gone
to heaven, and he seemed satisfied.

I passed that well about two years later
in the spring, and there was lupin growing
out between the boards, and the sweetest smell
was in the air, not like lupin at all.

The River God

From the last outpost of the setting sun,
where the delta meets the evening mist,
the River God plans a maid's abduction
and leads her weeping to an eerie tryst.

With bony hand he stroked her velvet hips
and left her shaken in his icy wake,
then as he leaned to kiss her frozen lips
he drew her windward to a shallow brake.

Now fish, now man,
he altered in her view,
his eyes were wild and yellow
then suddenly turned blue,
his hair was white and curling
then limp and blackened through.

He bound her fast with willows
against his scaly side,
then washed her face with kisses
as if she were his bride,
nor could she stay his passion
until the dim night died.

When dawn came sweet and creeping,
long had she ceased her weeping
and from that weedy cove where silence fell
she watched him vanish in the river's swell....

The Ballerina

Her dance begins, cold at first, with her dark
eyes closed, awaiting the transposition
of her flesh to fire. Figurations spark
somewhere in the zone of definition.
Her right foot floats out gracefully, in hope
to make the point perceptive, then down, down
to touch the polished floor, to interlope
upon the stage in waves of whirling gown.
The cold turns warm, turns flame, while music lifts
the dancer from the given and the real
into an atmosphere where movement shifts
and joins the universe of her ideal:
A pirouette becomes complete delight
when spirit's one with air and flesh in flight....

The Drowning

He swam past the surf to grasp her hand
and felt her icy fingers slipping free.
He clutched again and caught a ragged strand
of gold hair, long and streaming in the sea.

The strong current of the tide tumbled him
beneath the waves; he rose and gasped for air.
She was near him, reaching out with pale slim
arms, her sad blue eyes filling with despair.

As she coiled around him, all became clear.
There was a thud against his thigh and pain
as he went under, steeped in holy fear;
she was half-fish, a sailor's dreaded bane.

And far below, the last scene in his sight
was golden hair and sad blue eyes, and night.

City Park

I watched them through the elms in the park,
a ruddy boy tossing a beat-up ball
to his dog, content in the happy lark
of unmeasured joy and time. He would call
the mutt to his knee, pat his head, then toss
again, cheering on his pal to final victory.
The dog would trot back proudly to his boss,
drop the wet lump, then stop to scratch a flea.
They ran and jumped and wrestled on the grass
till the sun went down, and when the first star
began to shine, the boy made a last pass
and sailed the ball above the elms, so far
their bit of magic vanished out of sight:
Not boy or dog would find it in the night.

Mary Cathcart

In the old iron-gated cemetery in our village,
there is an unfamiliar name etched on stone:
"Mary Cathcart," it faintly reads, and gives her age
beneath the moss as twenty-one. She is not alone.

Underneath her date of death, eighteen ninety-four,
deeper still within the moss it reads, "and child."
They lie in the steep downhill corner for the poor,
unkempt, but filled with lupins running wild.

I go there sometimes, in the late red
of evening, when the blaze of sun settles down
behind the hills, as if drawn to the granite head-
stone of Mary and the child. I often frown,

puzzled by her brief and fettered life,
and wonder if she died in some disgrace,
perhaps in childbirth, with only a midwife
to hear her cry, to bathe her feverish face.

No loving hand to give her courage to persist?
No one to mitigate the rising thrusts of pain?
How my mind does wander—unable to dismiss her
or commiserate, unable to abstain....

At Devil's Point

Across the prairie haze he saw a kid
on foot and nudged his sorrel to pursue
the distant shape, but it jumped like a wild
animal, quick and furtive, out of view.

He sucked in hot noon air and his great chest heaved
as he kicked his sweating horse up the trail,
reining close in to the thickets leading
to Devil's Point along a rocky sill.

That hazy shape brought the misery back;
nights he couldn't sleep, his drunken stupors,
all burning, swimming back, and for what,
an empty poke that didn't last the night.

His squint eyes scanned the deserted prairie,
vast and still, not a soul to see him tremble,
remembering the kid he'd shot and buried
years ago. He headed down into the brambles.

A rattler got him, folks in town all said,
and mourners prayed for his immortal soul.

Black Bird

Nobody heard the young girl cry
As she leaped from the rocky cliff,
But we have wondered since her death
What silent misery could have driven her so.

Only a black bird in the sky,
Hovering over the rock she fell upon,
Perhaps heard a plaintive sigh
As she ended it all.

For that same bird still circles
That stark cliff and the rock below,
Crying, crying into the gray sky
As if he too would die.

The Deserted Garden

He bowed his head and blessed the small green
seeds as he popped them into the ground.
They would sleep like children, deep and serene
in the crumbling soil piled in soft mounds.
Each day he stood guard over the garden
until he felt part of himself rested
with the seeds below. He was their warden,
one in whom their flower fate was vested.

He watched in winter while the garden slept,
armed the beds with peat against the snow.
But in the slanting rain the dark seeds crept
secretly beneath the fence, inching slowly
toward the promised sun, leaving their host
deserted, puzzled, and listless as a ghost.

An Afternoon Encounter

They sat in the park on a wooden bench,
each watching the courthouse clock;
a stranger would have known they were strangers,
he a tall young man, she a fair young woman.

He glanced at her appreciatively.
She glanced uncertainly toward the lake.
He retreated. They watched two swans swim by.
He offered casually, "Warm afternoon."

She, softly, "Yes, the swans have found the shade."
He, bravely, "There's a bench under that oak."
She, with spirit, "Oh, yes, it does look cool."
Together they trekked through the tall damp grass.

Two hours passed as happily they talked.
They failed to note the chiming of the clock.

Plainsland

Scattered across the Texas plains
were the deep canyons, rutted and ribbed
to a dry-bed floor, chomping bits
of red clay in their ancient mouths.

Above, chaste clouds gazed hazily
into the pitted earth, so far below
their kinship seemed unlikely.
And on the deserted plain, tumbleweeds

tumbled endlessly where no tree stood
to break their mindless run to an abyss.
But always came the faint stir of horned
toad and snake, cruising through the parched grass.

And at night, legions of planets agape
looked down in reverence on this mound
of sister-sod as they hung in abeyance
on a spirit tree of luminous dust.

The Innocent Witch

Seen through rain, the house discouraged entry,
blinds were drawn, dark windows shuttered fast.
She donned her favored clothes along with grief,
still loving all the ghostly things she wore,
all befitting the persona she bore in life:
a crucifix of pearl, two large jet rings,
a flowing robe dipping to the floor.
A raven and two black toms had been sent
to the vet for destruction, her last wish.
Now, nothing living remained in the house,
except her fey spirit which seemed to breathe
through naked walls.
              She had read omens,
predicted her own death by sudden fire,
set the date in December at the solstice.
She had fancied herself a modern witch,
knew black magic, peered into the future
through a crystal ball, delved into evil,
believed that resurrection from the pit
would guarantee her immortality.
She was prepared when lightning struck.
Poor innocent, trusting the old devil
to honor pacts and bring her back intact;
thus zealously he baits the mortal trap.

Domestic Storm

Outside the sky cracked wide and thunder fell,
fell shivering and shattered panes of glass,
fell through the brick and split the chimney wall
invading like a beast from hell below.

Rain snaked its way across the wooden floor,
came lapping through the curtains wrung with rage,
then settled thirstily beneath her chair.

An evil in the house conspired with storm
to send her tumbling in the light-struck room.

From underneath the ground began to heave,
while ceiling muttered through the shaking roof.
She felt an angry presence watching her,
felt him peering through the walls, a menace
quite malign, stalking round the darkened house.

A door began to open of itself,
then lightning flashed and lit his face:
His haunted eyes implored her to remember
that quarrels served to motivate surrender.

The Young Swan

Gentle cygnet, find contentment in the pool
where insubstantial shadows drift, water
whispers flow and misty beams enchant.

In the woods den, hear the alder limbs cry out
in green ecstasy, lauding your tender form
where lineaments of hope spring to the fore
and summer's ivory nectar glints your wings.

Nor shall the moon know promise such as yours,
drifting now like a token thing, but soon,
soon to gather glory in the sun.

Though hidden now in your enfolded wings,
your sweet days will be. Come, feathered light
from the still, soft shade, pluck destiny
and soar, wild one, above my head in passing....

Winter Kill

On the far white hill, a snow-encrusted
beast was glittering in the moonlight,
moaning wildly, plunging his hoof
into the icy drifts. He was caught
in a steel trap set by a hunter.
His great head shook as he lunged
against the cold contraption,
an evil thing to him that stole his right
to ply the winter fields for food.
He would die there in the trap,
the forest whispered it to him.

— *Part Two* —

"Befriend us, Time, Love's gaunt executor!"

(Robert Graves, *In Time*)

The Moon Rode High

The moon rode high as we began
To choose our weapons for their strength,
I drew my distance from you, man,
And you from woman, length for length.

The moon rode high above the hills,
Our swords were crossed, then swiftly thrust,
Each found their mark, each struck to kill,
Each plunged with full and blooded lust.

Our swords fell red-stained on the green.
When all was done, we yet did live,
And naked stood we in-between
The need to die, or all forgive.

Your wounded self was not unknown,
It looked to be as dire as mine,
Two creatures cast in flesh and bone,
Each cut from one impure design.

The moon descended in the west
And love breathed low in faint relief,
Was then the bloody green was blest
For man and woman, found in grief.

The Cliffs

Behind the white dunes,
they lay in quiet peace
while the high heat of noon
burned on the distant sea.

They heard the breakers sweep
up to shore, a gull cried
a lonely sound that ceased
then echoed on the cliffs.

They waited for the moon
to light their pathway up
and felt the sudden chill
of night on the summit.

The dangerous path,
dark and unforgiving,
circled twice around
a rugged stone.

The waves rolled in to boom
against their pinnacle
shouting their thunder,
the underside of noon.

The Cold Breath

It is long past time for us to reassess
the cold breath of familiarity
hanging between us as a cruel reminder
of the first strangeness we no longer possess.

Or, is the heart deceived by the passing days
into the calm of false security;
does it feel, as in the last second of drowning,
the watery bliss of floating in the waves?

Soul Mates

Beyond nose and mouth and ears.
beyond tongue, beyond brain,
beyond the reach of mortal tears,
your Self eludes my claim.

When I approach its semblance
and feel my longing sear,
reposing in your tender glance
Love's lineaments are clear.

Sea Zone

Into those locked years
he plunged through the wreck of days
to find the Sea of Memory.
She was there, holding fast,
in the lost Atlantis of his heart.

Debts

The first degree of love
is paid for on the card
and when the debt falls due
the interest must be charged.

He should have weighed the cost
experience would run,
when all the bills add up,
it seems a tidy sum.

Dictionary World

Under special signs & symbols in the dictionary,
I found a round O under biology,
Meaning lacking or absent, as a part.

So if I sigh a series of O's,
You may take it to mean
In your absence I am destitute.

How could I know your love was not to last?
You were mine, and I had given all,
Content that you would always feel the same.

Until I found that parts could be lacking or absent.
Now I brood and search for the lost magic symbol
To restore a sign of meaning to my dictionary world.

Windless Summer

When will the wind begin again?
Will it blow down from the hills
pine-scented from the tallest trees?
I scarcely breathed this summer past,
no air moved down the sound from sea
and breathless lay the town.

    Since William died
no thoughts can fly among the clouds;
their folded wings beat futilely
from where they hide, waiting
for wind to hurl them back to sky.
but all is still and unbecoming
with leaning day, lank and open
       to a windless way....

Portent

Somewhere, beyond times ending,
Camelot waits, still tending
Dreams we did not comprehend, held for us
In trust, joy portending.

Love's Antidote

What black magic would it take,
Poison from Love's deadly snake,
A potion to kill this ache, strong enough
For thirst I cannot slake?

Kiss Me Kate

Kiss me until I smother,
Not like sister or brother
Nor doting mother, then I will promise
To be your sweet other!

Haven't We Met Before?

Pardon me, but haven't we met before?
Was it Paris, on top of the tower
when you came out the elevator door
wearing a blue dress, I think, a flower
in your hair? Strange we should meet again
after so many years, and quite by chance.
You are as lovely now as you were then,
has it been three years since that week in France?

You were to phone me before I left town,
I seem to recall. I waited all day,
long past train time, then ran all the way down
to your hotel: You had been called away.
Forgive me, I don't want to seem a bore,
but I must know, haven't we loved before?

Love Bane

Love is anxiety and madness.
Only the strong have stomach
to bear its compilation of pain.

Better to be done with it!

But then, I feel a great
flutter of resignation:
Love is here to stay.

Visitor

Though in delirium, I seem to recall
it was September when we met.
The sun shone on your face,
or did it shine from behind....
You must forgive my lapse of memory,
for I am ill, they say.

It was noon, was it not?
(Or should I say there was no time,
nor place, nor anyone but you;
how my breath stopped.)
They tell me now the end is soon,
but, I do remember you—and noon.

Love-Knot

— 47 —

When tracking through the mist of days
to find the place where first we met
(in long relief of fated encounter),
we stumbled on the hour-rope of time,
now healed in a Gordian Knot of love

Warning

O, Cyna, heed my words:
You drift toward disaster,
You run to him with wild
Blossoms in your hair,
A scent disguise to hide
Your feigning heart.

Sweet Wind

Sweet wind cleaving to the snow,
Press down whitely on her feet,
Leave her dancing in the glow
Moon leaves glancing on the street.

Sweet wind flicking in the night,
Blow through teasing in her hair,
Weave your ribbon round her bright,
Keep her gently in your care.

Sweet wind freezing all the boughs,
Blush her lightly on her face,
She has made a marriage vow,
Teach her keening to embrace.

Child of Love

Come into my heart, my love,
Where time shall cease.
Feel the passing moment halt
Where silence dwells.

No sun shines here,
Nor does the bird sing,
Only a voiceless Spring hangs
Pure and waiting in the air.

Oh, see—silence is a child of love,
Though no eye nor ear it bears,
We know its presence to be there.

Oh, yes, my love, the silence speaks
Soft syllables we cannot spell,
When silence knows…and does not tell.

— *Part Three* —

This thing of darkness I acknowledge mine.

(Shakespeare, *The Tempest*)

Epitaph

Into the hushed darkness
all must go,
past fancies and dreams,
past fears and lies,
all must go that dies.

Angel-in-Waiting

O Sir, is the hunter within you
weary and filled with despair?
Has your fine steed flagged
but a breath from the fount
and left you faint with thirst?

Descend from your mount.
Lie here beside me on the grassy crest
and I shall carry water and sprinkle
icy drops upon your lips.
Lie here beside me, and rest.

In this solemn shade,
tell me of the fords you crossed,
tell me of the scars you bear,
tell me of the causes won and lost.

O Sir, will you not speak?
Will you not hold my hand
in the darkness and pour your
sorrow into this holy silence?

O Sir, you sleep, do you dream?
All I ask is but a morsel of your breath
delivered in a kiss—a morsel of your life
in courage spent upon this worldly plain:
Do you deny me this?

Ah, you wake, and light is stirring deep
within your eyes—you reach to touch me
through the whorl of time…and you are mine.…

At Gettysburg

The earth had heaved with dead at Gettysburg
where stiffened men half buried in the woods
were humped in death like stones, row on row,
while in the distance generations grieved.

In daylight now we pause to remember
the earth, where wretched men screamed their pain
before we pledged it to be neatly tended.
We dare to breathe again, when sad ground is green.

Descension

I shall drink
only where the lily pads
float on crystal water,
where underneath,
unseen eyes
watch me skim between
reflecting light
and the dark descending.

The Dust Catcher

The dust speaks to him. He listens.
The very old, the squalling new,
are specks to him. He knows their truth
in their first spark of life.

He has known the crowned heads
of nations, known sea captains,
doctors, actors, headhunters and gods;
on and on…specks. Only he remains
indestructible, like a black hole that
whiffs everything into a pail of night.

Ah, but such tales of power and beauty:
"Such pain and suffering, such lives lived in
phantasies that soothe and charge the spirit
for action, action that leads to love, hate,
remorse or wonder." All this he sees and more
in a grain of swirling dust.

But he remains a trustworthy agent, sworn
to justice and impartiality. It is
crucial to be gentle when performing his
function of disposal, always he retains
a speck's full essence and blends it
mightily with the spinning dance
of stars. Someday, you will know
he speaks truth, when you meet…
      face to face.…

Viola

For Viola Caroline Norsworthy
Born 19 December 1903. Died 10 December 1971.

Winter comes more somber than before,
Now that she sleeps
Where other seeds have slept,
In the cold brown earth.
Oh, purple mask of violets on the lawn,
Do you deceive me with your gentle mirth?
Is there a Spring beneath you there
Or is it Winter everywhere?

The Barrier

In a dream
I saw a landscape
Of primitive contortions.
Huge curling trees reached
Toward a cobalt sky
Where constellations swirled
In arches of golden light.

A great glass dome
Covered the mystic world
Locked in perfect silence;
But for my nails scratching
And my cries:
       let me in,
       let me in!

Spirits in Transit

Pale moon, they drift before you in a silent mass,
and all belong forever to the dead of night.
Their gaze is cast upon a waiting path
and you are now their only thread of light.
Pale moon, from your silver shadow where they wait,
lead uncreated creatures to their fate.

Lady of the Nettles

Lady of the nettles
Robed in flowing red
Cast your giant shadow
On the lily bed…

Use your thorns for needles
Sew my garment fast
Make the finest stitches
Bindings that will last…

Groom me for eternity
Put out my waning spark
Nothing must burn after
My journey through the dark.

Leave me with the lilies
When you have mended all
Spread your red robe flowing
On my catafalque.

Sophia and Ariel

In the vanishing light Ariel waits
silently with her dying charge.

Sophia: Will only pain tell me yet I live?
       Will I, quiet one, fall beneath
       the blade of my shallow deeds?
       Will you not forgive
       and lead me, old and wise,
       into the waiting continuum?

Ariel: Your frailties are not a question....

Sophia: Strange self, calm and at peace
       in your hushed darkness;
       you cling to nothing;
       only the harmonies of space
       reveal your hidden symmetry.

Ariel: Such music is my soul.

Sophia: I follow your melody
       through drifting mist—
       you lead me to a sunlit field.
       There, on the graves of my kinsmen,
       you call their spirits forth again,
       name by name, love by love.

A dream? Was I also buried there?

All, all shimmer away
and leave me stricken!   Alone....

Ariel: Only until clarity becomes
the final gift of being.

Sophia: I see...the clouds lift...

Ariel: Pure essence, such mystery
as you shall not be again.
You who are weak and strong,
who love and hate,
you who are mild and brave,
who knows both joy and sorrow,
you are the good and wise.

The wise who now have done
With all but light and self....

The Closed Door

What waits behind the door,
out of sight, but breathing
through? Something leans lightly,
taps against the panel door.

What entity waits there,
waits guarding, preventing
entry, where none may go,
behind the nether door?

To Dream

Once I dreamed
I was some other
perfect self,

a spirit,
an immortal being,
born of myth.

But the clock,
ticking the years away,
will not keep the lie;

nor will my sense,
locked in flesh and bone,
be traitor to my thought.

It is all very clear:
Time will carry me
to death. O dream!

Dark Angel

My wings are wide,
encompassing eternity—they glide
over the dreamer tossing,
lost on the shadowed crossing.

Know me by this:
Night will fall, softly as a kiss,
with my dark wings sweeping
all to my arms for keeping.

Full Circle

When you are divested
of all you hold dear,
shall you then know,
in that final breath of being,
the dark seed of your beginning?

— *Part Four*—

Ah Love! Could you and I with Him conspire
to grasp this sorry scheme of things entire
would not we shatter it to bits—and then
remould it nearer to the Heart's Desire!

(Omar Khayyám: *The Rubáiyát*)

The Fisherman
> *"There is no magic without belief."*
> *(Paul Valéry)*

Was it magic
when he fed the hungry crowd?
Did the loaves and fishes
fill their need for food:
Or, did the people hunger
for a different fare,
more precious than their minds
had need to prove?

Janus

Enter at your peril
On the moated tongue
To the other side.

Pass through the barrel
Bloated thick with young
To find the gems inside:

Here angels carol
Canticles strung
With pearls uncalcified.

Defiant Image

Defiant image, captured on a field of blue,
you stare intently from a wooden frame,
fixed in oil and thought; yet you overflow
to exceed the boundaries of canvas,
a just man, resolute, and a fighter.
Old honor, that protects old values held,
clings mightily, gives grudgingly to sway
of principles denying certitudes,
tradition and the tested. Enemy
of the shoddy, the dreadful and the slick,
you draw a battle line and sink your flag
to guard the ground where vanished legions bled.

On Occasion

On occasion
he has been known to check his greed,
he has displaced his good for another
and graciously accepted second best.

Only rarely
has he stolen the advantage,
given rein to a selfish ego,
denied a reasonable request.

Quite often
his little sins seem rather pale
measured against a cruel conscience
bent on a constant quest.

After all
is there not a point of wisdom
where one can accept imperfection
and share the human stigma with the rest?

Keepsake

In an old trunk
I found a lovely thing,
round and soft to touch,
I loved it very much.

I can't remember what
I did with it, but then
I'm sure it will pop up
when I need it once again.

Solicitude

Though I concur delight may be agreeable,
and mad desire delectable, indeed,
I find their presence never quite foreseeable
and often they desert in time of need.

I sometimes think a calm solicitude
extends more deeply to the inner man,
I cannot doubt the measure of its good
when senses tell it lives a longer span.

The Haunting

I do not see a spirit,
nor does a spirit speak to me,
but in my head a wistful voice
sings chapel-like refrains.

Am I haunted by the waif
who wandered through my childhood
and once saw Jesus in a garden?

Carolyn

She peeped at me from the corners
of her eyes, a winsome glance
unworldly wise. A child
scarcely three, but laying hold
of my hidden fantasy; do children
come from Faerie?

Sweet Demon

Sweet demon of my dream,
Sharing every morsel you possess,
Scoring out the sustenance of worth,
Bringing in the mead we will profess.

Sweet demon of my dream,
You know all I will allow,
You bring every given into birth,
And all that will be, hidden in the now.

Vixen

Vixen, gazing on your starving cubs,
there will be food tonight
for the sky is lit by crystal stars
shining on moonlit fields.

You who are wise and feed on fear
know the rewards of cool surveillance,
tonight, not even a mate detracts
from the necessary hunt.

While yelps hound you from your den,
prey far into the snowy woods,
weave deep through the frozen grass;
food shall be found tonight under the stars.

A Different Drummer

A different drummer plays for you,
I know you'll leave me soon,
You hear your name upon the wind
And fiddlers call the tune.

But in the drifting sands of time
Along your destined way,
You'll find me in your memory
And long for yesterday.

But I shall not be near you then
And I shall not regret
A different drummer played for me
And taught me to forget.

Alter-Ego

You may know her as Olivia,
I know her as Jane.
You may think her beautiful,
I know she is plain.

Nor does she have fine character,
as some at times suppose,
her faults are legendary
to those who really know.

Because she sleeps and sups with me,
in confidence we talk,
what she has said and done till now
would make a monkey balk.

But in my mirror every night,
We bid sleep well and douse the light.

Reality or Dream

Enthralled we live and weave our webs,
no more than spiders on a leaf
drinking the dew of flowers,
our elixir of reality or dream.

If I must give an edge to either,
let it be to dreams,
which are the faint, the fragile,
and more likely lost in the dark.

Our Natal Pact

We love, though love must end,
We laugh, though tears may come
To claim our laughter as their twin.
We plan, we build, we dream.
We let our fancies run as free
As blood when wounded to the quick.

Defeat is everywhere in every man,
Within our Natal pact—it waits
And still, we love, we dream
We hope that all be well.
Each day we all pretend again,
To keep the dark away.

The Creed of Mammon

Gather the little fishes in
to feed the birds of prey.
Gather the unsuspecting lambs
and fleece them in the lea;
grind their bones to silver ash
and package it to sell,
turn every bit of flesh to cash
and you will prosper well!

Salt

When ambition ran to glory
in his youthful days,
his dreams were pure and sweet,
what did he know of salt:
The story of his life was incomplete.

Now, in his after-youth,
the wounds of time run deep
and he has learned to stand alone
while salt becomes his wage:
Life's story lived is paid.

Entranced

Step outside your trance
and find the paradox of mind:
There is no salt or sweet
can lure us from propensity
for self-inflicted joy or pain.
We are judges on the bench
and weigh calamity as ill
when most denying motive
in our choice. Look in the glass,
see how the truth dissolves
and passes with your breath.